THE SATIRE LOUNGE

Joseph Hutchison

THE SATIRE LOUNGE

Joseph Hutchison

FOLDED WORD

Meredith

Requests for permission to make copies of any part of this work should be e-mailed to:

editors@foldedword.com, subject line "permissions"

ISBN-13: 978-1-61019-227-9

Folded Word
79 Tracy Way
Meredith, NH 03253
United States of America
WWW.FOLDEDWORD.COM

Cover art by Joseph Hutchison
Design by JS Graustein
Author Photograph by Melody Madonna
Titles and text set in Chaparral Pro

For Melody, who smiled when she read these poems

The Ph.D Candidate Contemplates His Future

Someday I'll retire and do nothing but write.
Bot-pomes and theories of theories about books
(if we haven't deep-sixed books by then)—
these shall be all my delight.
Between blog-poetics and shots of Patrón,
I'll watch my laptop's screenlight glint on the gilt
of my oak-framed diploma
and savor the aroma
of ganga wafting from my home office nook,
the smoke-curls swirling with the lilt
of something twelve-tone,
or Cage's "Suite for Toy Piano." The moon
shall incline her dirty cheek toward mine,
on Mike's Fine Sardines I shall dine,
I shall blow into a blue bassoon
or cough in green ink,
the pleasures of tenure misting my eyes.
If the weather's mild
I'll stagger with my flask like a toddling child
out into the yard
and flop on my back under stars—
pulsing stars that whirl as I toast the poetry wars
whose blitzkriegs made my reputation.
And there I'll snooze till sunrise
pinks my shut eyelids. I'll smile and think:
Oh, what adventures we had in the avant-garde!

THOUGHT POLICE

for Murray Moulding

As the critic drove, caught up in unpacking a scrap
of verse (did it not allude to Wittgenstein?), he
missed the light's turn and so never caught
sight of the city bus hustling to its next stop.
Now the jaunty firemen jabber as they scrape
the remains of him off the dash, and the 'copter
jabbers above the gawkers and TV reporters

who all jabber too—just as Wittgenstein jabbered
while shaking a fireplace poker at Karl Popper,
insisting there are no philosophical problems,
only linguistic ones (this a mere fifty miles
from war-rubbled London, when Hiroshima
and Nagasaki still lay flayed and smoking).
How all this jabber would distract our scholar

if he wasn't already heaped like raw sausage
in the throbbing sarcophagus of the ambulance.
He'll never remember those Theorists in shades
slouched against a red brick wall, gazing out
in canny silence over the accident scene—
Camels angled from their lips, fists in pockets,
faint smiles shadowed by the brims of their fedoras.

CONCEPTUAL WRITING

In the chipped blue bowl there are snippets of lettuce, the edges brown with an oysterish slime. Tough tomato wedges the color of sun-bleached orange plastic. Deliquescent cucumber slices. Carrot shreds curled and dry as the armpit hair of a carnival strongman. Dressing the consistency of industrial sludge.

We're hungry but reluctant, and in the end don't bother taking a bite. On the restaurant's comment card we write: "The salad you served was rancid, but the idea of it pictured on the menu was delicious."

To Poets Who Whine about the Inadequacy of Language

If you distrust words
so much, why not
shut up? Why waste
the sacrificed flesh
of trees, or strew your
anemic traces across
our computer screens
(each pixel lit by burning
400-million-year-old
ferns and trilobites,
or butchering big rivers
with the blades of turbines)?
You'd deplete the earth
to trumpet your faithlessness?
Why not simply learn
to paint, or play the flute,
or bow in bewitched
silence over a whirling
potter's wheel?
Words don't serve
because you won't serve
them. So: *Get thee hence!*
And don't let the sacred
door of the dictionary
hit you in the ass.

To Writing Programs: A Canticle

This way, that way, that way, this,
Here and there a fresh love is.

— Robert Herrick, "To Bacchus, A Canticle"

for Seth Abramson

[The following found poem stitches together 19 headlines
from ads for MFA programs published in the January/
February 2010 issue of *Poets and Writers*—an issue
focused on the theme of "inspiration." *Each sentence is
an actual headline, verbatim*—though headlines presented
in parentheses are not parenthesized in the actual ads.
Headlines are given in the same order as the ads appeared
in the publication, and the advertised programs are listed
in order of appearance after the poem.]

Realize the greatness
of your voice. Inspiration
comes in many forms.
Discover the writer's life
in New York City.
(You're not in Iowa
anymore.) Write

in Miami! Write
from the Heartland.
(We'll let our reputation
speak for us.) Write
from the heart
of writing. (The world's
focus is on our faculty.) My
words, my time, my MFA.
Otis emphasizes the writer's
ability to articulate
innovation. What makes
us different? Expect
more. Big thinking
for a big world.
Finally—an MFA
that trains you
for a career, not just
a genre. Study
your way. (Scribbling on
the ether.) Achievement!
Change the world
with words.

[1] *The Voices Summer Writing Workshop*

[2] *NYU School of Continuing and Professional Studies*

[3] *The New School*

[4] *Emerson College*

[5] *Florida Center for the Literary Arts at Miami Dade College*

[6] *Ashland University*

[7] *Warren Wilson MFA Program for Writers*

[8] *Lesley University*

[9] *Drew—The Caspersen School of Graduate Studies*

[10] *University of Nebraska at Omaha*

[11] *Otis College of Art and Design*

[12] *Pine Manor College Low-Residency MFA*

[13] *Queens University of Charlotte*

[14] *Chatham University*

[15] *Western Connecticut State University*

[16] *Burlington College*

[17] *Prague Summer Program of Western Michigan University*

[18] *The Rainier Writing Workshop at Pacific Lutheran University*

[19] *Antioch University Los Angeles*

Another Prize-Winning Poetry Collection

I don't know what's more humiliating: that I read it
through in one rapt sitting, grinning and grieving
in all the right places; or that I acquired it free
for review and still felt cheated—but nevertheless
slipped it into the bookcase beside a dozen more
hardbound and slickly jacketed volumes
by the same implacable scribbler.

Lighting a Cigar Beside the Public Works Trench

After Robert Bly's "Watering the Horse"

How strange to think of giving up all punctuation!
Suddenly I see with such clear eyes
the match's exclamation point as it flares
toward the hissing split in the muddy gas main!

Tinnitus

haiku writing dream:
cowflop swarmed by green-silk flies—
seventeen of them

Still Pond, Still Summer Night

small

    frog

        splash—

some

    kind

        of

foot

    note

        ?!

Poem Beginning with
Two Lines by Tom Montag

Poetry
bears repeating
because it bears on
and bears up
what we can't
bear to lose
but will—
unless I've completely
lost my bearings.

POSTCARD TO VAZAMBAM

for Vassilis Zambaras

Vassilis, I mean no slight,

saying you write light
verse. I mean, of course,

your light touch, bright-
ening glance and grin

as you knife a jolt of
lightning into the heart

of darkness. So quick,
I always think *How*

sweet as I bungee
into the mindfulness

beneath each last line
you love to dangle

us dazzled readers from.

PASTICHE

After The Unsubscriber
and Parts of a World

I like how Bill Knott blows his mouth harp
blithely, as Stevens played his oboe. I call
them masters as I hum-blow my kazoo,
spin these verses out of mere asides
signed *sotto mano* by deaf-mute twins
parted at birth, but years later delivered
into each other's care. Small wonder
my poems veer from rancor to abject
tenderness, marking over the years
a hidden rhythm like the heart of some
gravedigger scooping out vacancies
in the gathering dusk. Yet I (no Knott,
no Stevens) play whatever my little gift
allows, swaying in these masters' shadows.

RESPECT THE SIGNS

An Englishing of "Respete las Señales"
by Francisco Hernández

[I've had a lot of fun translating the poems of Méxican poet Francisco Hernández because he revels in wordplay. The stanzas of this poem, for example, are based on road signs commonly seen along Méxican streets and highways.]

Don't scatter poems
along the roadway.

Page left
is for overtaking.

Hendecasyllables
500 feet.

Yield
to changing stanzas.

Caution: sonnets
entering and exiting.

No passing when rhyme is continuous.

Urbane poetry:
speed restricted.

Don't damage the vowels.

Poems more than 10 lines long
must use expressway.

If you write, don't drive.

Caution: approaching next poem.

Slow: men writing.

Choose lane before poem narrows.

High-speed poetry
not allowed on this road.

Reduce the velocity
of your reading.

A ticket will be issued
to anyone trashing poetry.

U-turn in 250 verses.

UNCLES

A Thanksgiving poem

Uncle Walt drank German beer,
   Uncle Wystan whiskey.
Uncle Dylan drank whatever
   made his tongue feel frisky.

Uncle Pablo savored eels;
   Uncle Osip, stones.
Uncle Seamus—cabbage and sloes
   boiled with marrow bones.

Uncle Willie dreamed in a tower,
   Uncle Rob in a shack.
Uncle Wally dreamed at the office
   of peignoirs and birds that were black.

Uncle Bill loved many women,
   Uncle Frank loved men.
Uncle Jack loved anyone
   who'd stimulate his pen.

These and other uncles come
    to visit once a year.
We munch a roasted bird with them;
    they toast themselves and cheer.

In the living room we men doze off,
    beguiled by the loud TV.
The aunts who cooked the meal for us,
who drank and ate and dreamed with us,
    study us silently.

ALTER EGO

Man's life as commentary....

—Nabokov, *Pale Fire*

So this rival blogger eviscerates
my candid assessment of a certain
poseur gris whose late-life memoir
mentions me, but mixes me up
with another drunk student poet
babbling Yeats in the bottle-strewn
corner of an almost famous dive
on South Dubuque Street, Iowa City.
How, I ask, could I let it go? How
was I to know the poser's my rival's
brother, who lost his legs in a freak fall
from some tree house he'd years ago
climbed into with his lady love and six
Daffy Duck tabs of acid? My good name
was at stake (all right—my *username*),
so I posted a mention of the poser's
back-then-well-known addiction
to certain sex acts involving a rope,
and failing to think things through
also mentioned his lover's name—
the mother, it turns out, of his three

clueless children who still make time
to visit him twice a month in prison.
How could I have known these saints
are my rival's nephews and nieces?
Mistakes were made. But was it right
for him to detail my indiscretions
online—using my legal name? Who
in the world does he think he is?
Not that it matters. What matters is
I know where he lives. How often
I've knelt on the midnight lawn
outside that craptacular bungalow
he blogs in—which stands, ironically,
one block over and two doors down
from mine—squashing my nose
against his window to watch him
tap tap tapping in a Marlboro haze!
Then last week I finally got it—
what had to be done. I lined up
a dozen fresh eggs on my kitchen
window sill, and now they're perfect
for a drive-by one of these nights,
one of these stifling summer nights
when Iowans leave their windows
open, though any wide-eyed cicada
might clack in. Maybe the neighbor's
cat hops in with a mouse in its jaws.

Or maybe there's a sudden storm
of stinking egg grenades. As I sprint
for my idling car, I'll shout, "A terrible
beauty is born, asshole!" Of course,
I hope he'll be struck by enlightenment
like a zen student the master slaps,
and realize how wrong old Auden was
when he wrote my rival's favorite quote
(he crams it into every other post):
"Poetry makes nothing happen."

THE BLOGGER ON WHY
HE SHOULD NEVER DRINK

Last night I fumbled for my love
poem's bra-latch while kissing
each feminine rhyme, drenching each
enjambment in my Irish whiskied breath,
when suddenly my nightmare zipper
popped, and what should poke
out but a rifle barrel? Something
high caliber—something automatic.
Just then the title of my next red-faced
rant came to me: "Power Politics
and the Death of Pleasure."

SUBTEXT

I can only half believe
the mind is merely
thinking meat, although
one day I did glimpse
the *glovedness* of my hand—
a numb moment teeming
with incipient losses:
hidden bones laid bare,
blood, lymph, nerves,
muscle and fat and skin
all melting down to muck:
gone, the whole subtext
of yet one more unfinished
experiment in consciousness—
like this little machine
made of words....

THE POET TENDERS HIS APOLOGIA IN TERMS
HE HOPES HIS SON WILL UNDERSTAND

My love for poetry,
I tell him, goes back
to a kids' cartoon.
Rocky and Bullwinkle.

Right, he says.

Really! Rocky
the Flying Squirrel
and his sidekick,
Bullwinkle J. Moose,
find themselves lost
in a desert. The sun's
broiling, sky white.
They're crawling.
Their red tongues
drag the sand. Then
this tall dune rises
in front of them,
and a thought bubble
pops up, tied to both
their heads: a palm tree
bends inside it, over
cool blue water.

It's too much! They
scramble to the top,
but on the other side—
no oasis. Not even
a twist of cactus.

Empty desert,
he says. I get it.

But he doesn't,
so I tell him: Now
the narrator speaks up.
William Conrad!
You know—classic
voiceover artist?
Radio's Matt Dillon.

Matt Dillon, I almost
hear him thinking.
Something About Mary.

Gunsmoke, I explain.
Before James Arness.

He sighs, my son.

Well—imagine it,

I say. Conrad's voice
booming like God's.
*Our heroes looked out
over miles and miles
of miles and miles.*

I let the words drift
off into the sheer
openness of childhood.

Not *his* childhood,
though. He gives me
a quick, pinched look,
shakes his head.

Poetry, I shrug.
He rolls his eyes, and I'm
moved to repeat (with
more emotion
than either of us likes):
Poetry!

THE SATIRE LOUNGE

(A muse walks into a bar...)

Did she ever dream you'd still be here?
Bowing down to the scarred oak bar,
wiping up swill and beer-nut skins
in the same stained apron you wore
years ago when you first met—you,
a guileless guy from Nowhere Town,
sweeping tips into a college fund;
her from the coast (the coast of what
she'd never say). One heady dose
of her incomparable wandering voice
and all you could think was: *Out
of my league.* Now here she is
after all this time, and you can't
manage a fond hello—because it all
comes flooding back: the cramped
attic at the top of the stairs; the john
whose faux chrome faucets leaked
a rusty *koto* music day and night;
the low-slanted ceiling where plump
roof rats scratched and squeaked.
Flaws that didn't seem to phase her.
What she noted were the raw pine
bookshelves propped on cinderblocks

(her backhanded praise: "They sag
with promise"). She liked the little desk
too, so narrow it hugged your knees.
You'd lean there toward a red sunrise,
yield to the rush of images her presence
called up, and jot them down, then
hour by hour refine, refine. Later on,
she'd lean in close and you'd recite,
bowed to wavering candlelight (as Keats,
you'd tell her, must have done it; "Oh yes,"
she'd say, with a distant look). You'd roll
each sweet word on your loving tongue
like a warm caramel. And if the next day
your poem seemed tasteless, each line
a long awkward walk off a short cliché—
well, you knew she'd bring you more.
But no. Not for ages. Now here she sits,
or one with her very own knowing glance,
bright enough to make you take the risk.
You plant your elbows on the bar, lean
toward her shining gaze. "Hey," you say,
"what's your pleasure?" Her smile is easy,
teasing, so you add, "You look familiar."
She draws a fingernail across your hand's
parchment skin and says: "I'd like to be."
It never fails. You pour a *gratis* glass
from the owner's private stock of good

Greek reds, and soon you're weaving back
to the padlocked shed for another bottle,
when suddenly you look up: the night sky's
this boundless star-field, all tingling fire,
and you're all *ah-hah* and blood-flow heat.
But once inside again you see she's gone,
who never did see an evening through.
You should close up, go home and pour
her visit into words, although it seems
another life when you could do such things.
So you linger on instead, downing shots,
swabbing the checkerboard linoleum
in the twitchy, neon jukebox glow. Time
and again you spin up "Walking the Floor,"
swinging your mop in a two-step stagger,
stroking the wood, hands like gloves,
dancing her absence to the end of love.

About the Author

JOSEPH HUTCHISON, author of 16 poetry collections and translator of Miguel Lupián's *Ephemeral* (also from Folded Word), lives in the mountains southwest of Denver, Colorado, the city where he was born. He teaches at the University of Denver's University College, where he directs two programs: Arts & Culture and Global Affairs. In September 2014, he was appointed to a four-year term as Colorado Poet Laureate by Governor John Hickenlooper. To learn more, please visit him at:

WWW.JHWRITER.COM

More from the Author

Thread of the Real
2012, Conundrum Press

Marked Men
2013, WordTech Communications

Bed of Coals
2014, FutureCycle Press

The Earth-Boat, 2nd Edition
2015, Folded Word

Ephemeral
(translation of work by Miguel Lupián)
2015, Folded Word

Acknowledgements

All except for the title poem first appeared — sometimes in early, untitled "notebook" versions — on the author's blog:

The Perpetual Bird
http://bitly.com/PerpetualBird

The author would like to thank himself for his steadfast support over the years.

The author and publisher would also like to thank Rose Auslander, Casey Murphy, Barbara Flaherty, Miran Reynolds, Maryka Gillis, Megan Graustein, and Alycia Nardini for their assistance at the press during the production of this chapbook.

More from the Folded Family

The Road to Isla Negra
by William O'Daly
with art by Galen Garwood

Hints
by Rose Auslander

Catherine Sophia's Elbow
by Darla K. Crist

What Was Here
by Julie Warther
with calligraphy by JS Graustein

For a complete list of our titles plus multi-media presentations from this book, visit the Folded Word website: WWW.FOLDEDWORD.COM

To report typographical errors or problems with the functionality of this book, email:

EDITORS@FOLDEDWORD.COM

Want more information about our books, chapbooks, and zines? Want to connect with contributors from this book? No problem. Simply join us at a social media outlet near you:

weblog: FOLDED.WORDPRESS.COM

Facebook: WWW.FACEBOOK.COM/FOLDEDWORD

Twitter: TWITTER.COM/FOLDEDWORD

We love to hear from our readers. Just send your thoughts via email to editors@foldedword.com with the subject line "SATIRE Feedback."

Cheers!

CPSIA information can be obtained at www.ICGtesting.com
Printed in the USA
LVOW08s1132010616

490689LV00006BA/168/P